PREFACE

1. Scope

This publication provides doctrine for religious affairs in joint operations. It also provides information on the chaplain's roles as the principal advisor to the joint force commander (JFC) on religious affairs and a key advisor on the impact of religion on military operations. It further provides information on the chaplain's role of delivering and facilitating religious ministries in joint operations.

2. Purpose

This publication has been prepared under the direction of the Chairman of the Joint Chiefs of Staff (CJCS). It sets forth joint doctrine to govern the activities and performance of the Armed Forces of the United States in joint operations and provides the doctrinal basis for US military coordination with other US Government departments and agencies during operations and for US military involvement in multinational operations. It provides military guidance for the exercise of authority by combatant commanders and other JFCs and prescribes joint doctrine for operations, education, and training. It provides military guidance for use by the Armed Forces in preparing their appropriate plans. It is not the intent of this publication to restrict the authority of the JFC from organizing the force and executing the mission in a manner the JFC deems most appropriate to ensure unity of effort in the accomplishment of the overall objective.

3. Application

a. Joint doctrine established in this publication applies to the Joint Staff, commanders of combatant commands, subunified commands, joint task forces, subordinate components of these commands, the Services, and combat support agencies.

b. The guidance in this publication is authoritative; as such, this doctrine will be followed except when, in the judgment of the commander, exceptional circumstances dictate otherwise. If conflicts arise between the contents of this publication and the contents of Service publications, this publication will take precedence unless the CJCS, normally in coordination with the other members of the Joint Chiefs of Staff, has provided more current and specific guidance. Commanders of forces operating as part of a multinational (alliance or coalition) military command should follow multinational doctrine and procedures ratified by the United States. For doctrine and procedures not ratified by the United States, commanders should evaluate and follow the multinational command's doctrine and procedures, where applicable and consistent with US law, regulations, and doctrine.

For the Chairman of the Joint Chiefs of Staff:

DAVID L. GOLDFEIN, Lt Gen, USAF
Director, Joint Staff

- **Clarifies the chaplain's advisement role in the targeting process to ensure the focus is on the ethical, moral, and religious dimensions.**

- **Expands the definition of religious advisement to include the potential impact of military operations on the religious and humanitarian dynamics in the operational area.**

- **Revises guidance regarding religious support during defense support of civil authorities operations.**

- **Expands the functions of chaplains supporting geographic combatant commands.**

- **Clarifies guidance for religious support and advisement during detainee operations.**

- **Clarifies guidance regarding chaplains maintaining confidentiality of communications when providing ministry to non-US Armed Forces personnel.**

- **Removes all references to the former United States Joint Forces Command and transfers responsibility for religious affairs functions to the joint staff chaplain.**

Intentionally Blank

TABLE OF CONTENTS

Intentionally Blank

EXECUTIVE SUMMARY
COMMANDER'S OVERVIEW

- **Presents the basics of religious affairs, the authorities for chaplains, noncombatant status of the chaplain, and combatant status of enlisted religious support personnel.**

- **Describes the fundamentals, relationships, and duties involved in religious affairs.**

- **Addresses the roles of religious affairs in joint operations; to include chaplain liaison in support of military engagement.**

Basis of Religious Affairs

US military chaplains represent specific religious organizations and work together within the pluralistic context of the military to ensure freedom of religion within the joint force.

The Services maintain chaplaincies to accommodate religious needs, to provide religious and pastoral care, and to advise commanders on the complexities of religion with regard to its personnel and mission, as appropriate. As military members, chaplains are uniquely positioned to assist Service members, their families, and other authorized personnel with the challenges of military service as advocates of religious, moral, and spiritual well being and resiliency.

Authorities

Military commanders are responsible to provide for the free exercise of religion of those under their authority as directed by Joint Publication 1, Doctrine for the Armed Forces of the United States.

Title 10, United States Code (USC), Sections 3073, 5142, and 8067, provides for the appointment of officers as chaplains in the Army, Navy, and Air Force. The Navy directs its Chaplain Corps to provide chaplains for the Marine Corps, the Coast Guard, and the Merchant Marine. Chaplains have rank without command (Title 10, USC, Sections 3581, and 8581), and function in the dual roles of religious leader and staff officer. Department of Defense Instruction 1300.17, *Accommodation of Religious Practices within the Military Services,* describes the commander's responsibility for religious accommodation.

The Noncombatant Status of the Chaplain

Article 24 of *Geneva Convention for the Amelioration of the Condition of the Wounded and Sick in Armed Forces in the Field* (sometimes referred to as Geneva Convention I) identifies chaplains as protected personnel in their function and capacity as ministers of religion. Service regulations further prohibit chaplains from bearing arms and classify chaplains as noncombatants.

The Combatant Status of Enlisted Religious Support (RS) Personnel

Enlisted religious support (RS) personnel, Army or Air Force chaplain assistants (CAs), and Navy religious program specialists (RPs) are combatants and, therefore, are without special protected status.

Fundamentals, Relationships, and Duties

Fundamentals

Religious affairs consist of the combination of RS and religious advisement. Throughout planning and execution commanders and their staffs consider the possible impact of religion throughout the operational area and area of influence. Chaplains and enlisted RS personnel assist the combatant commander and subordinate joint force commanders (JFCs) by enabling the expression of faith or religious practice for all assigned personnel. As a special staff officer, the chaplain advises the commander and other staff members on moral and ethical decision making, on morale as affected by religion, and personal issues.

Functional Descriptions

Religious support teams (RSTs), comprised of chaplains and their enlisted RS personnel, strengthen community life by delivering training and education to Service members and other authorized personnel.

Chaplains execute the commander's religious affairs program through religious advisement and providing RS. **Religious advisement** is the practice of informing the commander on the impact of religion on joint operations. **RS** includes:

- The provision and facilitation of religious worship, pastoral counseling, and Department of Defense support to accommodate the free exercise of religion for all authorized personnel.
- Advising the JFC on ethical and moral issues, and morale, as affected by religion.
- Pastoral care, counseling, and coaching which attend to personal and relational needs.

Service, Inter-Service, and Joint Relationships

The **Chiefs of Chaplains of the Military Departments** ensure active duty and reserve component chaplains and enlisted RS personnel are trained and equipped to provide RS when required, in support of combatant command (CCMD) requirements. The **Director, National Guard Bureau Office of the Chaplain (NGB-OC)**, directs, oversees, develops, and implements activities of the NGB-OC for the Chief, National Guard Bureau. The **Joint Staff (JS) Chaplain** advises the Chairman of the Joint Chiefs of Staff and the JS, and assists the CCMD chaplains. A joint force chaplain (**JFCH**) position is established at the CCMD, the subordinate unified command, and joint task force (JTF) level of command. The JFCH is the principal advisor to a commander on religious affairs. The **JTF chaplain** is the principal advisor to the commander on RS and is a key staff contributor on religious advisement. **Service and functional component command chaplains** are responsible for coordinating with the CCMD chaplain and delivering RS to personnel assigned or attached to the component command. **Service component command chaplains** advise the Service component commander on issues that are Service specific.

Functions

JFCH functions may include:

- Advising the JFC and staff on all matters of religion, ethical and moral issues, spiritual well-being, and morale, as affected by religion;
- Supervising assigned staff in order to communicate command religious priorities, assess and direct religious affairs activities, answer specific religious inquiries, facilitate unity of effort, and enhance lines of communication and situational awareness;
- Preparing RS portions of plans and annexes and participating in identifying religious affairs requirements during crisis action planning; and,
- Seeking opportunities to train religious support teams (RSTs) in related tasks identified.

Religious Affairs Throughout Levels of War

The JFCH is responsible for coordinating religious affairs and the employment of RSTs as necessary to accomplish the assigned mission. Religious affairs requirements vary at the tactical, operational, and strategic levels of war.

Enlisted RS Personnel Roles and Responsibilities

The Army or Air Force CA or the Navy RP provides enlisted support to the chaplain. The RS senior enlisted leader (SEL) is the principal enlisted advisor to the command chaplain. Services train their respective CA/RP to work directly within their Service chaplaincy prerogatives. The skills vary by Service and mission set. The JFCH and RS SEL understand the service-connected tasks and structure the delivery of RS to maximize the differences into a cohesive, seamless program of support.

Religious Affairs in Interorganizational Coordination

When directed by the commander, the JFCH establishes relationships with organizations in order to enhance capabilities. A JFCH's responsibilities to coordinate religious affairs for issues and activities for a JFC with multinationals might be expanded based on multinational agreements.

The Roles of Religious Affairs in Joint Operations

RST Participation in Military Engagement

Religious affairs in joint military operations will require a variety of actions supporting different types and phases of operations. Types of operations supported include: noncombat operations; combat operations; peace operations; stability operations; foreign humanitarian assistance; noncombatant evacuation operations; detainee operations; personnel recovery; mortuary affairs; and homeland defense and defense support of civil authorities.

Chaplain Liaison in Support of Military Engagement

Chaplain liaison in support of military engagement is any command-directed contact or interaction where the chaplain, as the command's religious representative, meets with a leader on matters of religion to ameliorate suffering and to promote peace and the benevolent expression of religion. It is a focused and narrow role that addresses religion in human activity without employing religion to achieve a military advantage. Chaplains involved in chaplain liaison maintain dialogue with indigenous religious leaders, communities, nongovernmental organizations, intergovernmental organizations, and other actors as directed by the commander.

CONCLUSION

This publication provides doctrine for religious affairs in joint operations. It also provides information on the chaplain's roles as the principal advisor to the JFC on religious affairs and a key advisor on the impact of religion on military operations. It further provides information on the chaplain's role of delivering and facilitating religious ministries in joint operations.

CHAPTER I
BASIS OF RELIGIOUS AFFAIRS

> *"Religious affairs are the commander's responsibility and consist of the combination of religious support and religious advisement. Religious support addresses the joint commander's responsibilities to support the free exercise of religion by members of the joint force....Religious advisement addresses the commander's requirement to receive germane subject matter advice on the impact of religion on operations."*
>
> **Joint Publication 1, *Doctrine for the Armed Forces of the United States*, 2013**

1. Introduction

a. Chaplains served with American forces in the colonial militias of the 1600s and have remained an integral part of the US military since the formation of the Continental Army and Navy in 1775. US military chaplains are a unique manifestation of the nation's commitment to the values of freedom of conscience and free exercise of religion proclaimed in her founding documents. US military chaplains represent specific religious organizations and work together within the pluralistic context of the military to ensure freedom of religion within the joint force.

b. The Services maintain chaplaincies to accommodate religious needs, to provide religious and pastoral care, and to advise commanders on the complexities of religion with regard to its personnel and mission, as appropriate. As military members, chaplains are uniquely positioned to assist Service members, their families, and other authorized personnel with the challenges of military service as advocates of religious, moral, and spiritual well-being and resiliency. Uniformed chaplaincies are essential in fulfilling the government's, and especially the Department of Defense's (DOD's), responsibilities to all members of the Armed Forces of the United States.

2. Authorities

a. The US Constitution, law, and policy support the free exercise of religion. For example, Title 10, United States Code (USC), Sections 3073, 5142, and 8067, provide for the appointment of officers as chaplains in the Army, Navy, and Air Force. The Navy directs its Chaplain Corps to provide chaplains for the Marine Corps, the Coast Guard, and the Merchant Marine. Chaplains have rank without command (Title 10, USC, Sections 3581 and 8581), and function in the dual roles of religious leader and staff officer. Department of Defense Instruction (DODI) 1300.17, *Accommodation of Religious Practices within the Military Services,* describes the commander's responsibility for religious accommodation.

b. Military commanders are responsible to provide for the free exercise of religion of those under their authority as directed by Joint Publication (JP) 1, *Doctrine for the Armed Forces of the United States.* Religious support (RS) to the personnel of each Service is the responsibility of their Service component commander with the joint force commander (JFC) providing guidance and oversight. Department of Defense Directive (DODD) 1304.19, *Appointment of Chaplains for the Military Departments,* establishes DOD policy that requires the Services to appoint chaplains to support commanders. It states, in part, that chaplains shall "serve as the principal advisor to commanders for all issues regarding the impact of religion on military operations." DODI 5100.73, *Major Department of Defense Headquarters Activities*, directs that all major headquarters (HQ), including joint HQ, provide for the management of religious affairs within the organization.

3. The Noncombatant Status of the Chaplain

Article 24 of *Geneva Convention for the Amelioration of the Condition of the Wounded and Sick in Armed Forces in the Field* (sometimes referred to as Geneva Convention I) identifies chaplains as protected personnel in their function and capacity as ministers of religion. Service regulations further prohibit chaplains from bearing arms and classify chaplains as noncombatants. As noncombatants, chaplains must not engage directly or indirectly in combatant duties; will not conduct activities that compromise their noncombatant status; must not function as intelligence collectors or propose combat target selection; and will not advise on including or excluding specific structures on the no-strike list or target list. Advisement will focus on the ethical, moral, and religious dimensions of the targeting process. Consistent with their noncombatant status, chaplains participate in operation planning and advise the command and staff on matters as appropriate; advise on the religious and humanitarian status of the command's operational environment (unless restricted by the law of war); provide input as to what constitutes religious structures or monuments of antiquity in a particular operational area; and, when authorized and directed by the commander, serve as a point of contact and liaison for local civilian and military leaders, institutions, and organizations, to the extent that those contacts relate to the religious or humanitarian purposes approved by the commander. See Articles 4, 6, 7, 9, 10, 11, 24, 28, and 47 of the Geneva Convention (I) for more information regarding treatment of chaplains in the context of the Convention.

4. The Combatant Status of Enlisted Religious Support Personnel

Enlisted RS personnel, Army or Air Force chaplain assistants (CAs), and Navy religious program specialists (RPs) are combatants and, therefore, are without special protected status. They are trained to use lethal force effectively and appropriately. Service doctrine defines their role as combatants. Additionally, the chaplain must be attuned to the issue of supervision of the enlisted support personnel to ensure their employment does not jeopardize the chaplain's protected status.

CHAPTER II
FUNDAMENTALS, RELATIONSHIPS, AND DUTIES

> *"The US Constitution proscribes Congress from enacting any law prohibiting the free exercise of religion. The Department of Defense places a high value on the rights of members of the Military Services to observe the tenets of their respective religions."*
>
> **Department of Defense Instruction 1300.17,**
> ***Accommodation of Religious Practices within the Military Services***

1. Fundamentals

a. Religious affairs are the commander's responsibility (see Figure II-1). Religious affairs consist of the combination of RS and religious advisement. The management of religious affairs requires fully informed and committed command support, communication, coordination, and collaboration. It is a mutual effort to create and sustain the most responsive and relevant service possible. It is built upon mutual respect and partnership from the combatant command (CCMD) and the Service component commands to the lowest level.

b. Throughout planning and execution commanders and their staffs consider the possible impact of religion throughout the operational area and area of influence. Religious beliefs and practices not only influence the adversary, they influence civilians and their

---

Religious Affairs

Chaplains Provide:

Religious Advisement

- Advice on impact of religion on joint operations.

- Advice on impact of military operations on the religious and humanitarian dynamics in the operational area.

- Advice on worship, rituals, customs, and practices of US military personnel, international forces, and the indigenous population.

- Liaison functions with officials of interagency, nongovernmental and interorganizational entities, multinational forces, and local religious leaders (when directed).

Religious Support

- Provision and facilitation of religious worship and pastoral support for all authorized personnel.

- Advice to the joint force commander on ethics, morals, and morale.

- Pastoral care, counseling, and coaching that reinforces spiritual strength and levels of commitment to increase resiliency of the force.

Figure II-1. Religious Affairs

---

societies within the operational area and may even impact the ideology or functioning of the government.

c. Chaplains and enlisted RS personnel assist the combatant commander (CCDR) and subordinate JFCs by enabling the expression of faith or religious practice for all assigned personnel. They also guard against religious discrimination of any kind within the command. Commanders are responsible for the religious accommodation of joint force personnel. Chaplains, assisted by enlisted RS personnel, provide for religious worship, rites, sacraments, ordinances, and ministrations. They also help leaders to implement programs to support individuals in sustaining optimal well-being and the capacity to carry out the mission as part of total force fitness.

For additional details on total force fitness, see Chairman of the Joint Chiefs of Staff Instruction (CJCSI) 3405.01, Chairman's Total Force Fitness Framework.

d. As a special staff officer, the chaplain advises the commander and other staff members on moral and ethical decision making, on morale as affected by religion, and personal issues (e.g., relational concerns, predeployment and post-deployment family counseling, and memorial observances). Additionally, based on the particular knowledge and experience of the individuals, and consistent with their noncombatant status, chaplains may advise the commander and staff members on various religious dynamics within the operational area. On occasion, chaplains may also be tasked with accomplishing certain liaison functions that relate to religious or humanitarian purposes approved by the commander, particularly with indigenous religious leaders and faith-based nongovernmental organizations (NGOs) operating in the operational area. Commanders should ensure that such tasks do not create the appearance of favoring a particular religion or compromise a chaplain's noncombatant status as described in Chapter 1, "Basis of Religious Affairs," paragraph 3, "The Noncombatant Status of the Chaplain."

2. Functional Descriptions

Religious affairs describe the JFC's responsibility to understand the role of religion as it affects the range of military operations and to provide for the free exercise of religion for authorized personnel. Chaplains execute the commander's religious affairs program through religious advisement and providing RS described as follows:

a. **Religious advisement** is the practice of informing the commander on the impact of religion on joint operations to include, but not limited to: worship, rituals, protected places, customs, and practices of US military personnel, international forces, and the indigenous population; as well as the potential impact of military operations on the religious and humanitarian dynamics in the operational area. Chaplains provide religious advisement consistent with their noncombatant status.

For more information, see Appendix A, "Religious Estimate."

b. **RS** consists of:

(1) The provision and facilitation of religious worship, pastoral counseling, and DOD support to accommodate the free exercise of religion for all authorized personnel. JFCs should be advised that when chaplains provide incidental ministry to non-US Armed Forces personnel, chaplains are required to preserve confidential communications in the same way such communications are preserved with US Armed Forces personnel.

(2) Advising the JFC on ethical and moral issues, and morale, as affected by religion. In the performance of the chaplain's primary duties of religious accommodation and pastoral care, the chaplain may offer advice to the commander regarding the chaplain's unique perspective and role as a religious ministry professional.

For further information on the qualifications of religious ministry professionals, refer to DODI 1304.28, Guidance for the Appointment of Chaplains for the Military Departments.

(3) Pastoral care, counseling, and coaching which attend to personal and relational needs. This includes relational counseling by chaplains which may be enhanced by their proximity and immediate presence, distinguished by confidential communication, and imbued with professional wisdom and genuine respect for human beings. Such counseling is most effective when based on strong relationships developed in the context of shared life in the same unit. Some examples of care are: work-space visitation, coaching on military life, pre- and post-deployment training for Service members and their families, crisis prevention and response, family life programs, memorial observances, and combat casualty care. Religious support teams (RSTs), comprised of chaplains and their enlisted RS personnel, strengthen community life by delivering training and education to Service members and other authorized personnel.

c. **An RST** is a team comprised of at least one chaplain and one enlisted RS person that works together in designing, implementing, and executing the command religious program. The members of an RST may come from the same or different Service components.

3. Service, Inter-Service, and Joint Relationships

a. **Military Departments.** The Chiefs of Chaplains of the Military Departments provide advice to the Secretaries of the Military Departments and Service Chiefs as they carry out their respective Title 10, USC, responsibilities for organizing, training, and equipping US military forces. Although the Military Departments are not part of the chain of command for joint US military operations, the Chiefs of Chaplains can provide joint force chaplains (JFCHs) with significant reachback capabilities and expertise in religious affairs. The Chiefs of Chaplains ensure active duty and reserve component chaplains and enlisted RS personnel are trained and equipped to provide RS when required, in support of CCMD requirements.

b. **Armed Forces Chaplains Board (AFCB).** The AFCB consists of the chief and deputy chief of chaplains from each of the military departments. In accordance with DODI 5120.08, *Armed Forces Chaplains Board,* the AFCB advises the Secretary of Defense (SecDef) on religious, ethical, and moral matters for the Services. The AFCB also advises SecDef on the following policy matters: the protection of the free exercise of religion;

acquisition, professional standards, requirements, training, and assignment of military chaplains; all RS providers; procurement and utilization of supplies, equipment, and facilities for religious use; promotion of dialogue with civilian organizations regarding religious issues; and promotion of joint military endeavors for the delivery of ministry by the Services throughout DOD whenever practicable.

c. **The National Guard (NG) Bureau** is a joint activity of DOD. The Director, National Guard Bureau-Office of the Chaplain (NGB-OC), directs, oversees, develops, and implements activities of the NGB-OC for the Chief, National Guard Bureau (CNGB). The Director, NGB-OC, serves as a principal advisor to the Service Chief of Chaplains on religious matters relating to the NG. NGB-OC supports the CNGB as an advisor to the CCDRs on NG religious affairs that pertain to the CCMD missions, support planning, and coordination for activities as requested by the Chairman of the Joint Chiefs of Staff (CJCS) or the CCDRs. NGB-OC is the channel of communications for all religious matters pertaining to the non-federalized NG among DOD components, the several states, and territories. The military response to extraordinary events that require defense support of civil authorities (DSCA) will be a coordinated effort between the NG in state active duty or Title 32, USC, and Title 10 or Title 14, USC, forces. NG RSTs, under the supervision of commanders and in coordination with the National Guard joint force headquarters-state (NG JFHQ-State) chaplain, will normally be the first military RSTs on the scene during a catastrophic incident. The NG JFHQ-State coordinates RS with the NGB-OC. However, once federalized, RSTs are under the operational control of the JFC and receive guidance from the JFCH.

d. **The Joint Staff (JS) Chaplain** advises the CJCS and the JS on, and assists the CCMD chaplains with, the following:

(1) The constitutional free exercise of religion and related matters impacting DOD, the JS military personnel, and their families.

(2) The dynamics of religion and potential mission impacts across the range of military operations.

(3) The integration of RSTs into joint force organizations in order to coordinate defense-wide RS.

(4) Religious, moral, and ethical issues related to policies, programs, initiatives, exercises, and operations.

(5) CCMD religious affairs priorities, in coordination and consultation with the command chaplains of the CCMDs.

(6) Religious aspects of functional policy and joint operations, in coordination with the Office of the Secretary of Defense through the AFCB and the Service Chiefs of Chaplains.

(7) Review of all JPs for religious affairs relevancy and accuracy.

(8) Advisement regarding CCMD RS requests for forces (RFFs) and individual augmentees (IAs) submitted via the Global Force Management process.

(9) Coordination with Service force providers for meeting special, CCMD short-term RS requirements such as seasonal religious needs.

(10) Support of joint training integration into Service chaplain schools, based on emergent doctrine and operations.

(11) Coordination of educational opportunities for joint-level RST members.

(12) RST participation in joint exercises worldwide, as appropriate.

(13) The collection, analysis, and organization of joint RS lessons learned for integration into joint doctrine, training, and education initiatives.

(14) Provision of pastoral care to the JS and the Office of the CJCS.

e. A JFCH position is established at the CCMD, the subordinate unified command, and joint task force (JTF) level of command. The JFCH is the principal advisor to a commander on religious affairs. The JFCH is a member of a commander's personal staff and reports directly to the commander. The JFC should normally select the senior chaplain from the joint force to be the JFCH, who may or may not be from the JFC's own Service. The JFCH issues coordinating guidance to subordinate component commanders and chaplains under the authority of the commander to optimize RS within the joint force. Services and Service components retain authority for managing religious affairs within their forces, subject to the policy of the CCDR and the coordinating guidance of the JFCH.

f. The functional CCMD chaplain provides advice to the CCDR and staff on religious affairs specific to the command's mission. The functional CCMD chaplain is a personal staff officer, supported by an appropriate staff section of RST personnel, who:

(1) Provides strategic- and operational-level advice and situational awareness for the CCDR and staff on all matters related to religion, ethics, and morale.

(2) Engages with senior military chaplains, government officials, officials of NGOs and intergovernmental organizations (IGOs), and local religious leaders as directed by the CCDR.

(3) Exercises functional supervision over the administration of RS within the command.

(4) Reviews available religious affairs capabilities for supporting command missions, and recommends the allocation of religious resources to prevent or eliminate unnecessary duplication and overlap of functions among supporting RS assets.

(5) Oversees the collection of religious lessons learned from supporting RSTs and the distribution of religious lessons learned to joint and Service repositories.

g. The JFCHs supporting the geographic CCMDs manage RS with both a strategic and operational emphasis. The role of the geographic CCMD chaplain mirrors that of the JS chaplain with a specific focus on joint operational issues pertaining to their area of responsibility (AOR). JFCHs also supervise the RS aspects of the theater security cooperation programs within their AORs and coordinate the management of RS among subordinate unified commands, JTFs, and functional and Service components, as approved by the geographic combatant commander. The geographic CCMD chaplain is a personal staff officer, supported by an appropriate staff section of RST personnel, who:

(1) Provides strategic- and operational-level advice and situational awareness for the commander and staff on all matters related to religion, ethical, and moral issues, and morale, as affected by religion.

(2) Engages with senior military chaplains, local and national religious leaders, and others, as directed by the CCDR.

(3) Develops, reviews, and revises RS appendices to theater plans, orders, and directives.

(4) Coordinates and guides components to align with the theater campaign plan and established corresponding religious affairs goals and objectives.

(5) Builds joint and multinational RST interoperability and capacity through exercises, training events, and subject matter expert exchanges.

(6) Plans for crisis and contingency response in-theater.

(7) When requested or directed by the commander, assists with the development of professional chaplaincies in militaries in the AOR in support of building partnership capacities in the areas of good governance, human dignity, and religious freedom.

(8) Exercises functional supervision over the administration of RS within the command.

(9) Reviews available religious affairs capabilities for supporting command missions, and recommends the allocation of religious resources to prevent or eliminate unnecessary duplication and overlap of functions among supporting RS assets.

(10) Oversees the collection of religious affairs lessons learned from supporting RSTs and the distribution of those lessons learned to joint and Service repositories.

(11) Coordinates with NGB-OC State Partnership Program leadership for unity of effort.

h. The JTF is the most common type of joint force command established to accomplish a specific mission in a geographic area or perform a particular function. The JTF chaplain is the principal advisor to the commander on RS and is a key staff contributor on religious advisement. The JTF chaplain is responsible for requesting, coordinating, and providing RS for the JTF, including coordinating with commanders regarding the employment of RSTs as necessary to accomplish the assigned mission.

For a more detailed discussion of CCMD, subordinate unified command, and JTF organizations, responsibilities, and functions, see JP 1, Doctrine for the Armed Forces of the United States, *and JP 3-0,* Joint Operations.

    i. Service and functional component command chaplains are responsible for coordinating with the CCMD chaplain and delivering RS to personnel assigned or attached to the component command.

        (1) A functional component is normally, but not necessarily, composed of forces of two or more Military Departments. Functional components include the joint force air component commander, joint force land component commander, joint force maritime component commander, and joint force special operations component commander. A functional component command chaplain, like a JTF chaplain, is the principal advisor to the functional component commander on religious affairs. The functional component chaplain coordinates with the CCMD chaplain.

        (2) Service component command chaplains advise the Service component commander on issues that are Service specific. In addition, the Service component chaplain coordinates with the CCMD chaplain and appropriate JFCH on all matters that relate to the component command's supporting mission.

4. Functions

    General. Joint RS requirements are determined and validated in accordance with existing joint processes. RSTs need to be well-integrated into their staffs and must use command reporting and tasking procedures. Chaplains must understand the limits of their tasking authority. Official tasking comes from appropriate command authority. Chaplains do not normally task subordinate chaplains directly.

    a. Figure II-2 shows conceptually how the chaplain's tasks differ in a joint environment in relationship to the echelon the chaplain is serving. The more senior a chaplain, the more the chaplain functions as a staff officer and functional manager of religious affairs for the JFC, rather than as a direct provider of RS.

    b. The JFCH assists the JFC in addressing the ambiguity and uncertainty of religious affairs in a complex operational environment. Thus, the JFCH assists in planning as it applies to the integration of religious affairs in joint operations. Religious affairs planning is based on the situation and is detailed, systematic, and continuous.

    c. **JFCH Functions**

        (1) **Advise.** The JFCH advises the JFC and staff on all matters of religion, ethical and moral issues, spiritual well-being, and morale, as affected by religion. Consistent with their noncombatant status, chaplains also advise the JFC and staff on matters pertaining to the ethical/moral implications of command plans, policies, operations, and strategies to

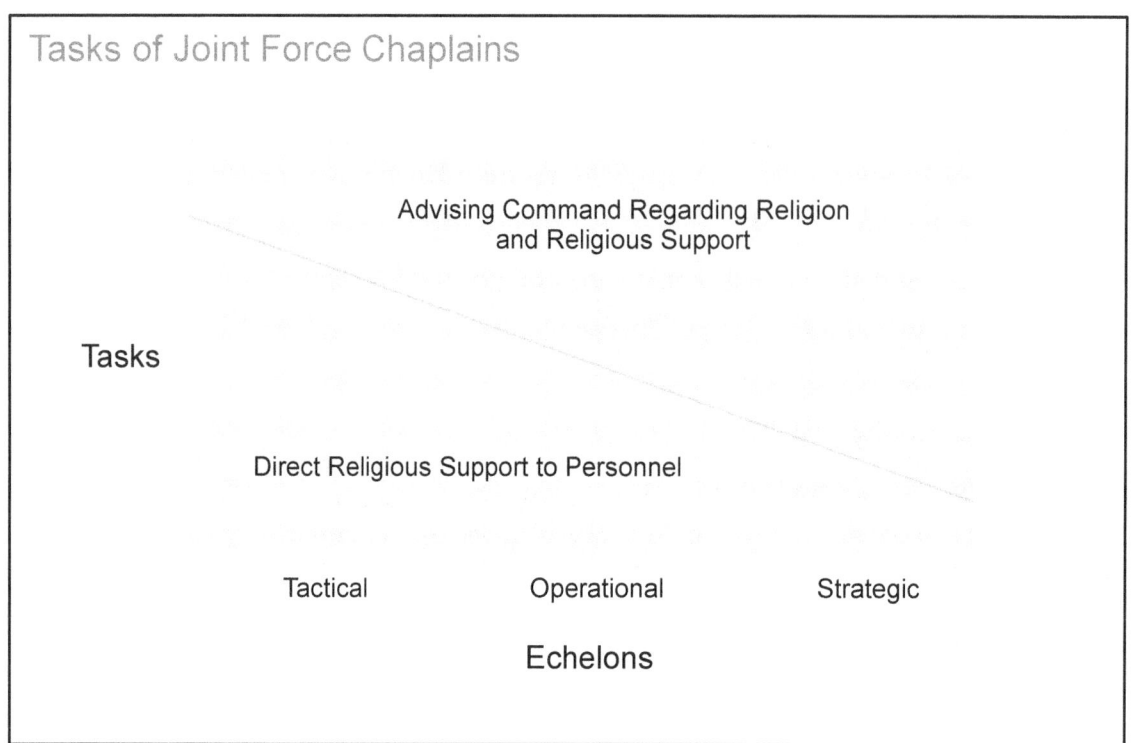

Figure II-2. Tasks of Joint Force Chaplains

include advice on the impact of operations on religious and humanitarian dynamics in the operational area. The JFCH advises subordinate JTF RSTs on the conduct of religious affairs.

For more information, see Appendix A, "Religious Estimate."

(2) **Supervise.** The JFCH supervises assigned staff in order to communicate command religious priorities, assess and direct religious affairs activities, answer specific religious inquiries, facilitate unity of effort, and enhance lines of communication and situational awareness. The JFCH also provides functional oversight and guidance to subordinate JTF RSTs.

(3) **Plan.** The JFCH prepares RS portions of plans and annexes and participates in identifying religious affairs requirements during crisis action planning. The JFCH ensures that required RS capabilities are identified and included in the command RFFs and request for IAs.

(4) **Train.** The JFCH seeks opportunities to train RSTs in related tasks identified in Chairman of the Joint Chiefs of Staff Manual (CJCSM) 3500.04, *Universal Joint Task Manual* and amplified in the *Joint Mission-Essential Task List*. (See Field Manual [FM] 7-15, *Army Universal Task List*; Air Force Doctrine Directive 1-1, *Air Force Task List*; Chief of Naval Operations Instruction 3500.38; Marine Corps Order 3500.26; and US Coast Guard Commandant Instruction 3500.1B, *Universal Naval Task List*.)

(5) **Resource.** The JFCH identifies RS materiel, force structure, and facilities requirements. The JFCH plans chaplaincy force structure to meet force deployment requirements, special religious holidays, and sacramental duties; the JFCH integrates these RS forces requirements in the CCDR's RFFs. The JFCH coordinates with appropriate legal agencies to develop responsive methods to receive and acknowledge private donations, mailings, and unique religious articles. The JFCH recommends command policy for the decommissioning of sensitive religious articles, clothing, chapels, and the return of such items to the sustainment base.

5. Religious Affairs Throughout Levels of War

The JFCH is responsible for coordinating religious affairs and the employment of RSTs as necessary to accomplish the assigned mission. Religious affairs requirements vary at the tactical, operational, and strategic levels of war (see Figure II-3). Decisions made and actions executed at one level can impact others.

a. Examples of responsibilities at the strategic level include:

(1) Advising the CCDR on religious affairs affecting the command.

(2) Coordinating the provision of RS with JS, Service, JTF, and multinational force command chaplains as appropriate.

(3) Engaging with senior military leadership, government officials, NGO and IGO officials, and national religious officials as directed by the commander and consistent with the chaplain's noncombatant status. Commanders should ensure that such tasks do not create the appearance of favoring a particular religion.

(4) Advising partner nation chaplains and senior military leadership on the development of their professional chaplaincies, as requested by chaplains of partner nations, in coordination with NGB-OC, and, as approved by the JFC.

(5) Preparing appropriate portions of theater plans, orders, and directives.

(6) Developing and recommending strategic command policy regarding religious issues.

b. Examples of operational-level responsibilities include:

(1) Advising the JFC on religious affairs affecting the operational area.

(2) Coordinating the provision of RS with higher, adjacent, and subordinate HQ command chaplains.

(3) Executing regional chaplain liaison initiatives in coordination with the CCMD chaplain and at the direction of the commander.

Religious Support Teams Integrated into Levels of War

Level	Unit	Involves	Area	Universal Joint Task List
Strategic National	Joint Staff	National policy development and national government-to-government interactions.	World	SN 4.3.2 Coordinate religious affairs.
Strategic Theater	Combatant Command	Regional military strategy, derived from policy that provides a framework for conducting operations.	Area of Responsibility	ST 4.2.5 Coordinate religious support.
Operational	Component	List the tactical employment of forces to national and military strategic objectives through the design and conduct of operations using operational art.	Joint Operations Area	OP 4.4.6 Integrate religious support.
Tactical	Division, Brigade, Combat Team, Regiment, Strike Group, Wing, etc.	Focuses on planning and executing battles, engagements, and activities to achieve military objectives assigned to tactical units or task forces.	Operations Area	ART 4.2.4 Plan religious support operations. MCT 4.6.2.2 Provide religious ministries support. NTA 4.4.5 Accommodate religious needs. AFTA 4.4.6.1 Provide religious observances. AFTA 4.4.6.2 Provide pastoral care. AFTA 4.4.6.3 Advise commanders on religious matters.

The three levels of war—strategic, operational, and tactical—help clarify the links between national strategic objectives and tactical actions.

Legend

AFTA	Air Force tactical task	OP	operational
ART	Army tactical task	SN	strategic national
MCT	Marine Corps task	ST	strategic theater
NTA	Navy tactical task		

Figure II-3. Religious Support Teams Integrated into Levels of War

(4) Engaging with regional senior military and religious officials consistent with their noncombatant status. Commanders should ensure that such tasks do not create the appearance of favoring a particular religion.

(5) Preparing RS portions of operation plans, orders, and directives.

(6) Developing and recommending operational command policy regarding religious issues (e.g., religious facility use, literature distribution, ecclesiastical correspondence and visitors, NGO, and humanitarian assistance).

c. Tactical RS is a Service component responsibility. Examples of tactical level responsibilities include:

(1) Advising the commander on religious affairs affecting the operational area.

(2) Providing, facilitating, and managing RS in coordination with higher, adjacent, and subordinate HQ command chaplains, to include RS to recovered isolated personnel.

(3) Preparing RS portions of unit-level plans, orders, and directives.

6. Enlisted Religious Support Personnel Roles and Responsibilities

The Army or Air Force CA or the Navy RP provides enlisted support to the chaplain. The RS senior enlisted leader (SEL) is the principal enlisted advisor to the command chaplain. Services train their respective CA/RP to work directly within their Service chaplaincy prerogatives. The skills vary by Service and mission set. The JFCH and RS SEL understand the service-connected tasks and structure the delivery of RS to maximize the differences into a cohesive, seamless program of support.

a. The RS SEL:

(1) Analyzes, manages, and executes diverse RS requirements.

(2) Advises RS enlisted personnel in subordinate organizations and their command's SELs regarding religious affairs issues and activities.

(3) Advises the command's SEL and staff.

(4) Supports operations, exercises, engagements, and outreach.

(5) Manages RS resources and sustainment.

(6) Integrates, coordinates, or provides security as required.

b. Additional skills may include:

(1) Functional knowledge regarding world religions and the religious dynamics of indigenous populations.

(2) Arranging opportunities to promote religious cooperation, understanding, and support.

(3) Developing and providing mentorship for emerging military chaplaincies.

(4) Coordinating efforts for formal regional military working groups and military-to-military programs advising senior level noncommissioned officers on the religious, moral, and ethical issues related to policies and programs.

7. Religious Affairs in Interorganizational Coordination

When directed by the commander, the JFCH establishes relationships with organizations in order to enhance capabilities, promote interoperability, and advise the commander in support of mission requirements. Issues of legality, permissions, collaborative tools, information sharing, and partnering with other governmental agencies or partner nations to meet religious needs should be considered. A JFCH's responsibilities to coordinate religious affairs for issues and activities for a JFC with multinationals might be expanded based on multinational agreements. Examples of interorganizational coordination are:

a. Interagency: Department of State (DOS), Federal Bureau of Investigation, and United States Agency for International Development (USAID).

b. Intergovernmental: United Nations, North Atlantic Treaty Organization, and African Union.

c. Multinational: America, Britain, Canada, Australia, and New Zealand.

d. Nongovernmental: International Red Cross/Crescent and World Vision.

e. Private Sector: nonpublic or commercial individuals and businesses, specified nonprofit organizations, most of academia, and other scholastic institutions.

f. Contractors.

CHAPTER III
THE ROLE OF RELIGIOUS AFFAIRS IN JOINT OPERATIONS

> *"An operational commander, however well trained in the military issues, who is ignorant of or discounts the importance of religious belief can strengthen his enemy, offend his allies, alienate his own forces, and antagonize public opinion. Religious belief is a factor he must consider in evaluating the enemy's intentions and capabilities, the state of his own forces, his relationship with allies, and his courses of action."*
>
> **Paul R. Wrigley, "The Impact of Religious Belief in the Theater of Operations,"**
> **Naval War College Review, Spring 1996**

1. Religious Support Team Participation in Military Engagement

Religious affairs in joint military operations will require a variety of actions supporting different types and phases of operations. Close coordination should be maintained among the RSTs of the CCMD, Service components, JTFs, and other subordinate units involved in joint military operations. In addition to the responsibilities described in Chapter II, "Fundamentals, Relationships, and Duties," the list below is meant to illustrate some of the special considerations that RST members should keep in mind; it is by no means an exhaustive list.

a. **Noncombat Operations.** There are many types of activities that commanders conduct outside of combat operations. RST involvement in such activities may include:

(1) Liaison and coordination activities throughout the operational area and with subordinate units in support of the commander's theater security cooperation program. This includes participation in humanitarian and civil assistance missions.

(2) When directed by the commander, establishing relationships with appropriate local religious leaders in consultation with the CCMD chaplain.

(3) As requested or directed by the commander and consistent with their noncombatant status, building and maintaining partnership capacity by assisting other militaries in establishing or improving their own military chaplaincies.

(4) Building relationships and collaborating with other government agencies, NGOs, and IGOs.

b. **Combat Operations.** Consistent with their noncombatant status and in compliance with restrictions set forth in the law of war, chaplains may be involved in one or more of the following activities before, during, and after combat operations:

(1) Planning and coordinating to ensure pastoral care and the provision or facilitation of religious worship for the spiritual well-being of the Service members.

(2) Caring for the wounded and honoring the fallen.

(3) Advising on appropriate chaplain liaison in support of military operations.

(4) Ensuring the JFC and staff understand the constraints and restraints, as defined by the noncombatant status of chaplains.

(5) Coordinating for RST replacements.

c. **Peace Operations.** Peace operations include peacekeeping, peace enforcement, peacemaking, peace building, military peace enforcement, and conflict prevention efforts. The RST supporting peace operations must understand the unique requirements of each kind of peace operation. RSTs will be involved in many of the activities mentioned in paragraph 1a, "Noncombat Operations."

See JP 3-07.3, Peace Operations, *for more information.*

d. **Stability Operations.** Stability operations can present some of the most challenging and complex ethical situations that commanders face. An essential component of stability operations is working effectively with the larger interagency community, especially the DOS and USAID. RSTs supporting stability operations need to understand the special requirements of such operations, and should consult DODI 3000.5, *Stability Operations*, JP 3-07, *Stability Operations*, and JP 3-57, *Civil-Military Operations.* In these circumstances RSTs pay particular attention to interagency coordination and to coordinating with the CCMD chaplain in advising the JFC on religious affairs.

e. **Foreign Humanitarian Assistance.** These operations are characterized by a crisis event and the limited time available for RST planning, preparation, and response. As an example, refugees, displaced persons, and evacuees may present special challenges.

For more information on foreign humanitarian assistance, see JP 3-29, Foreign Humanitarian Assistance.

f. **Noncombatant Evacuation Operations (NEOs).** When directed, the JFCH coordinates RS for US forces conducting the NEO, other participating forces, and evacuees as authorized.

For more information, see JP 3-68, Noncombatant Evacuation Operations.

g. **Detainee Operations.** Military chaplains do not generally provide direct RS to detainees. Should the JFC determine a requirement to provide direct military chaplain support to detainees, communications between the chaplains and the detainees will be privileged to the extent provided by evidentiary privilege rules and appropriate Military Department policies. The JFCH advises the JFC on the religious needs and practices of detainees. In addition, the JFC may direct the JFCH to assess and ensure the humane treatment of detainees.

See JP 3-63, Detainee Operations, *for more information.*

h. **Personnel Recovery.** When directed, the JFCH coordinates or provides RS for phase I and II reintegration of recovered personnel. Recovered personnel who request pastoral care or counseling from Service chaplains must be clearly advised that their communications with the chaplain, as a formal act of religion or matter of conscience, are privileged communications and confidential under Military Rules of Evidence, Rule 503(b).

See JP 3-50, Personnel Recovery, *for more information.*

i. **Mortuary Affairs.** When specific faith group guidance on interment requirements or mourning practices of multinational, adversary, or indigenous religious groups is required during joint operations, JTF personnel may consult with the nearest joint force or Service component chaplain.

For additional guidance on mortuary affairs, see JP 4-06, Mortuary Affairs.

j. **Homeland Defense (HD) and DSCA.** RSTs should understand the interrelationship between HD and DSCA operations, and anticipate the potential for transition between these missions or simultaneous HD and DSCA operations. RSTs should also consider how legal authorities and command responsibilities differ based upon mission, i.e., Title 32, Title 14, and Title 10, USC. RSTs should also address coordination and collaboration with interagency, multinational, nongovernmental, and faith-based partners in the planning process. RSTs anticipate, plan, equip, train for, and effectively respond to natural disasters; terrorist attacks; or chemical, biological, radiological, or nuclear events.

For an updated list of national and state disaster relief organizations, see the National Voluntary Organizations Active in Disaster *website at www.nvoad.org.*

(1) **HD.** US Northern Command and US Pacific Command are primarily responsible for the coordination of RS for HD. RSTs provide RS to forces conducting HD in the air, land, and maritime domains during the range of military operations. Regardless of the operation, RS tasks, plans, and execution are similar. RSTs will follow command direction, joint and Service policy, supervisory chaplain guidance, and legal counsel regarding permissible chaplain activities in HD operations.

For additional guidance, see JP 3-27, Homeland Defense.

(2) **DSCA.** RSTs may be colocated with the joint field office in the joint operations area in order to coordinate with the appropriate emergency support function organizations. During DSCA operations, the RST deploys for the primary purpose of providing RS to authorized DOD personnel. DSCA operations present unique challenges, including:

(a) Establishing parameters for interaction with non-DOD civilians.

(b) The potential for interaction with local, state, territorial, tribal, and federal law enforcement and emergency response personnel and/or their chaplains.

For additional guidance, see JP 3-28, Defense Support of Civil Authorities.

(3) **Legal Considerations.** RSTs deploy during DSCA operations for the purpose of providing RS to authorized Armed Forces personnel. The Establishment Clause of the US Constitution and current DOD legal guidance generally prohibit chaplains from providing RS to the civilian population, other than in specific emergency situations. RSTs will not normally provide RS to persons unaffiliated with the Armed Forces, absent explicit and unambiguous tasking from proper authority. Examples are traditional open worship services and authorized support to persons under the care, control, or custody of the Armed Forces. Chaplains, absent any explicit command prohibition to the contrary, may act in their personal capacity to provide incidental RS to persons not affiliated with the Armed Forces during the execution of an assigned mission. This support may be provided when the following four criteria (also known as "the four pronged test") are met:

(a) The support must be individually and personally requested in an emergency situation, where the need is immediate, unusual, and unplanned.

(b) The need must be acute. Acute needs are those which are of short duration, prone to rapid deterioration, and in need of urgent and immediate care. The necessary provision of "last rites" is the clearest but not the only example of such needs.

(c) The requested support must be incapable of being reasonably rendered by members of the clergy unaffiliated with the Armed Forces. Time, distance, and the state of communications may require such a determination to be made on the spot, by the chaplain, based on the information available at the time.

(d) The support must be actually incidental. Such support incurs no incremental monetary cost and does not significantly detract from the primary role of the RST.

Based upon the above four criteria for intervention, RSTs may assist mortuary operations and recovery personnel. See JP 4-06, Mortuary Affairs, for more information.

(4) **Family Assistance Center.** During catastrophic events, a family assistance center may be activated. RSTs in the family assistance center provide RS to authorized DOD personnel and coordinate with civilian religious care providers as directed or required.

See JP 3-28, Defense Support of Civil Authorities, for more information.

2. **Chaplain Liaison in Support of Military Engagement**

"During the Spanish American War, General John J. (Black Jack) Pershing, used his chaplain in the Philippines as a liaison with Catholic clergy in the north and Muslim leaders in the south in an attempt to ease hostilities."

"Military Chaplains as Peace Builders Embracing Indigenous Religions in Stability Operations," William Lee, et al., February 2006

---

a. In many situations, clergy-to-clergy communication is preferred by the indigenous religious leader. Military chaplains with the requisite knowledge, experience, and training/education have religious legitimacy that may directly contribute positively to the JFC's mission.

(1) Military engagement is the routine contact and interaction between individuals or elements of the Armed Forces of the United States and those of another nation's armed forces, or foreign and domestic civilian authorities or agencies to build trust and confidence, share information, coordinate mutual activities, and maintain influence.

(2) Chaplain liaison in support of military engagement is any command-directed contact or interaction where the chaplain, as the command's religious representative, meets with a leader on matters of religion to ameliorate suffering and to promote peace and the benevolent expression of religion. It is a focused and narrow role that addresses religion in human activity without employing religion to achieve a military advantage. These activities can take place during any phase of an operation and may have implications at all levels of operations. Some parameters for chaplain liaison in support of military engagement are as follows:

(a) Do not conduct chaplain liaison unless directed by the commander and in concert with commander's guidance.

(b) Do not compromise noncombatant status.

(c) Do not function as intelligence collector.

(d) Do not engage in manipulation and/or deception operations.

(e) Do not take the lead in formal negotiations for command outcomes.

(f) Do not identify targets for combat operations.

(g) Do not use these engagements as occasions for proselytizing.

(h) Commanders should be aware that when chaplains provide incidental ministry to non-US Armed Forces personnel, chaplains are required to preserve confidential communications in the same way such communications are preserved with US Armed Forces personnel.

(i) Chaplains should coordinate chaplain liaison with other staff and non-staff agencies of the command.

b. Chaplains involved in chaplain liaison maintain dialogue with indigenous religious leaders, communities, NGOs, IGOs, and other actors as directed by the commander.

Intentionally Blank

APPENDIX A
RELIGIOUS ESTIMATE

When developing the religious estimate, the JFC may receive assessments and input relative to religious advisement from various subject matter experts. Chaplains participate in the development of religious estimates consistent with their noncombatant status. The following considerations can be used to develop the religious estimate to be used in religious advisement.

1. How do US political goals for this situation interface with the religious sensibilities of the host nation concerned and the local communities in the operational area?

    a. How is the host nation affected by the religious preferences of regional neighbors or global religious perceptions and pressures?

    b. What host nation cultural religious perceptions or practices conflict with US positions on democracy, personal dignity, religious tolerance/pluralism, and separation of religion/state?

    c. How is the host nation's political and diplomatic process influenced by religious persuasion?

2. How does religious liaison facilitate the commander's intent, end state, and operation or campaign plan objectives?

    a. Which lines of operation and lines of effort can religious liaison support?

    b. What are the measures of effectiveness for religious liaison initiatives?

    c. How are the objectives of religious liaison communicated to other levels of command?

    d. How can US military policies in the host nation support or offend religious preferences?

    e. How can religious liaison be reinforced by interagency organizations, IGOs, or NGOs?

    f. What is the type, amount, and duration of religious liaison that the command will support?

    g. How do branches/sequels address ongoing operations and religious liaison? What is the chaplain's role in the plans and preparation? What accurate and timely advice can be offered? Where is the best information and wisdom to be found?

3. What religious practices (or religions) directly affect the host nation decision-making process?

4. How does religion affect the principles of law and justice?

5. How does religion affect the use of force, civilian and military?

6. How does religion affect reconciliation, treaties, and a sustainable peace? What host nation religious principles and practices are available?

7. How does religion affect economic prosperity, distribution of income, and religiously factored concepts of economic justice?

8. How does religion affect social structures: class, caste, tribe, region, and occupation?

9. What is the relationship between religion and freedom of communication? Access to media? Restrictions?

10. What is the relationship between the state and education? Does the state sponsor religious schools? To what extent is there control of access to education, success based on religious bias, teaching materials, licensure of teachers, and other religiously factored elements?

11. How does the state use mass media to regulate or promote religious access and content (television, radio, and internet)?

12. What religious entities or organizations are formally and informally recognized by the state?

13. What is the role of religious leadership? What is the extent of their influence?

14. What is the role of the US military with global, regional, and indigenous faith based organizations (e.g., missionary, church, and religious NGOs)?

15. What considerations are important in the interagency and joint force environments with regard to religious factors?

16. What is the impact of US and global media coverage of religious issues in the host nation and the region?

17. What are the ongoing religiously factored conflicts in the host nation? What is the level of repression of minority religious groups?

18. What is the impact of a US/multinational presence on the religious life of the area? Does it support religious freedom and values? Incite violence?

19. What skill sets do multinational forces chaplains bring to support religious liaison with host nation?

APPENDIX B
REFERENCES

The development of JP 1-05 is based upon the following primary references:

1. United States Laws

a. Goldwater-Nichols Department of Defense Reorganization Act of 1986.

b. Title 10, USC.

c. Title 14, USC.

d. Title 32, USC.

e. Title 50, USC.

2. Department of Defense Directives and Instructions

a. DODD 1304.19, *Appointment of Chaplains for the Military Departments.*

b. DODD 5100.01, *Functions of the Department of Defense and its Major Components.*

c. DODI 1000.01, *Identification (ID) Cards Required by the Geneva Conventions.*

d. DODI 1300.17, *Accommodation of Religious Practices within the Military Services.*

e. DODI 1300.19, *DOD Joint Officer Management Program.*

f. DODI 1304.28, *Guidance for the Appointment of Chaplains for the Military Departments.*

g. DODI 3000.05, *Stability Operations.*

h. DODI 5100.73, *Major DOD Headquarters Activities.*

i. DODI 5120.08, *Armed Forces Chaplains Board.*

3. Chairman of the Joint Chiefs of Staff Instructions and Manuals

a. CJCSI 1301.01E, *Joint Individual Augmentation Procedures.*

b. CJCSI 1800.01D, *Officer Professional Military Education Policy.*

c. CJCSI 3150.25E, *Joint Lessons Learned Program.*

d. CJCSI 3405.01, *Chairman's Total Force Fitness Framework.*

e. CJCSI 3500.01G, *Joint Training Policy and Guidance for the Armed Forces of the United States.*

f. CJCSM 3122.01A, *Joint Operation Planning and Execution System (JOPES), Volume I, Planning Policies and Procedures.*

g. CJCSM 3122.02D, *Joint Operation Planning and Execution System, Volume III, Time-Phased Force and Deployment Data Development and Deployment Execution.*

h. CJCSM 3130.03, *Adaptive Planning and Execution (APEX) Planning Formats and Guidance.*

i. CJCSM 3500.03D, *Joint Training Manual for the Armed Forces of the United States.*

j. CJCSM 3500.04F, *Universal Joint Task Manual.*

4. Joint Publications

a. JP 1, *Doctrine for the Armed Forces of the United States.*

b. JP 1-02, *Department of Defense Dictionary of Military and Associated Terms.*

c. JP 2-01.3, *Joint Intelligence Preparation of the Operational Environment.*

d. JP 3-0, *Joint Operations.*

e. JP 3-08, *Interorganizational Coordination During Joint Operations.*

f. JP 3-16, *Multinational Operations.*

g. JP 3-27, *Homeland Defense.*

h. JP 3-28, *Defense Support of Civil Authorities.*

i. JP 3-29, *Foreign Humanitarian Assistance.*

j. JP 3-33, *Joint Task Force Headquarters.*

k. JP 3-57, *Civil-Military Operations.*

l. JP 3-61, *Public Affairs.*

m. JP 4-06, *Mortuary Affairs.*

n. JP 5-0, *Joint Operation Planning.*

5. Army Publications

a. Army Regulation 165-1, *Army Chaplain Corps Activities.*

b. FM 1-05, *Religious Support.*

6. Navy Publications

a. Secretary of the Navy Instruction 1730.7D, *Religious Ministry within the Department of the Navy.*

b. Secretary of the Navy Instruction 1730.10, *Chaplain Advisement and Liaison.*

c. Navy Warfare Publication 1-05, *Religious Ministry in the Fleet.*

d. Chief of Naval Operations Instruction 1730.1E, *Religious Ministry in the Navy.*

7. Air Force Publications

a. Air Force Policy Directive 52-1, *Chaplain Service.*

b. Air Force Instruction 52-101, *Planning and Organizing.*

c. Air Force Instruction 52-104, *Chaplain Corps Readiness.*

8. Marine Corps Publications

a. Marine Corps Manual, *Chaplains and Religious Affairs.*

b. Marine Corps Warfighting Publication 6-12, *Religious Ministry Support in the USMC.*

c. Marine Corps Reference Publication (MCRP) 6-12B, *Religious Lay Leaders Handbook.*

d. MCRP 6-12A, *Religious Ministry Team Handbook.*

e. MCRP 6-12C, *Commanders Handbook for Religious Ministry Support.*

9. Coast Guard Publication

Commandant, United States Coast Guard Instruction M1730.4B, *Religious Ministries within the Coast Guard.*

Intentionally Blank

APPENDIX C
ADMINISTRATIVE INSTRUCTIONS

1. User Comments

Users in the field are highly encouraged to submit comments on this publication to: Joint Staff J-7, Deputy Director, Joint Education and Doctrine, ATTN: Joint Doctrine Analysis Division, 116 Lake View Parkway, Suffolk, VA 23435-2697. These comments should address content (accuracy, usefulness, consistency, and organization), writing, and appearance.

2. Authorship

The lead agent and the Joint Staff doctrine sponsor for this publication is the Joint Staff J-1 Office of Religious Affairs.

3. Supersession

This publication supersedes JP 1-05, 13 November 2009, *Religious Affairs in Joint Operations*.

4. Change Recommendations

a. Recommendations for urgent changes to this publication should be submitted:

    TO: JOINT STAFF WASHINGTON DC//J7-JE&D//

b. Routine changes should be submitted electronically to the Deputy Director, Joint Education and Doctrine, ATTN: Joint Doctrine Analysis Division, 116 Lake View Parkway, Suffolk, VA 23435-2697, and info the lead agent and the Director for Joint Force Development, J-7/JE&D.

c. When a Joint Staff directorate submits a proposal to the CJCS that would change source document information reflected in this publication, that directorate will include a proposed change to this publication as an enclosure to its proposal. The Services and other organizations are requested to notify the Joint Staff J-7 when changes to source documents reflected in this publication are initiated.

5. Distribution of Publications

Local reproduction is authorized, and access to unclassified publications is unrestricted. However, access to and reproduction authorization for classified JPs must be IAW DOD Manual 5200.01, Volume 1, *DOD Information Security Program: Overview, Classification, and Declassification,* and DOD Manual 5200.01, Volume 3, *DOD Information Security Program: Protection of Classified Information.*

6. Distribution of Electronic Publications

a. Joint Staff J-7 will not print copies of JPs for distribution. Electronic versions are available on JDEIS at https://jdeis.js.mil (NIPRNET) and http://jdeis.js.smil.mil (SIPRNET), and on the JEL at http://www.dtic.mil/doctrine (NIPRNET).

b. Only approved JPs are releasable outside the CCMDs, Services, and Joint Staff. Release of any classified JP to foreign governments or foreign nationals must be requested through the local embassy (Defense Attaché Office) to Defense Intelligence Agency, Defense Foreign Liaison/IE-3, 200 MacDill Blvd., Joint Base Anacostia-Bolling, Washington, DC 20340-5100.

c. JEL CD-ROM. Upon request of a joint doctrine development community member, the Joint Staff J-7 will produce and deliver one CD-ROM with current JPs. This JEL CD-ROM will be updated not less than semi-annually and when received can be locally reproduced for use within the CCMDs, Services, and combat support agencies.

GLOSSARY
PART I—ABBREVIATIONS AND ACRONYMS

AFCB	Armed Forces Chaplains Board
AOR	area of responsibility
CA	chaplain assistant
CCDR	combatant commander
CCMD	combatant command
CJCS	Chairman of the Joint Chiefs of Staff
CJCSI	Chairman of the Joint Chiefs of Staff instruction
CJCSM	Chairman of the Joint Chiefs of Staff manual
CNGB	Chief, National Guard Bureau
DOD	Department of Defense
DODD	Department of Defense directive
DODI	Department of Defense instruction
DOS	Department of State
DSCA	defense support of civil authorities
FM	field manual (Army)
HD	homeland defense
HQ	headquarters
IA	individual augmentee
IGO	intergovernmental organization
JFC	joint force commander
JFCH	joint force chaplain
JP	joint publication
JS	Joint Staff
JTF	joint task force
MCRP	Marine Corps reference publication
NEO	noncombatant evacuation operation
NG	National Guard
NGB-OC	National Guard Bureau-Office of the Chaplain
NG JFHQ-State	National Guard joint force headquarters-state
NGO	nongovernmental organization
RFF	request for forces
RP	religious program specialist
RS	religious support
RST	religious support team

SecDef   Secretary of Defense
SEL   senior enlisted leader

USAID   United States Agency for International Development
USC   United States Code

PART II—TERMS AND DEFINITIONS

combatant command chaplain. The senior chaplain assigned to the staff of, or designated by, the combatant commander to provide advice on religion, ethical, and moral issues, and morale of assigned personnel and to coordinate religious ministries within the combatant commander's area of responsibility. (Approved for incorporation into JP 1-02.)

command chaplain. The senior chaplain assigned to or designated by a commander of a staff, command, or unit. (JP 1-02. SOURCE: JP 1-05)

joint force chaplain. The military chaplain designated by the joint force commander to serve as the senior chaplain for the joint force. Also called the **JFCH.** (JP 1-02. SOURCE: JP 1-05)

religious advisement. The practice of informing the commander on the impact of religion on joint operations to include, but not limited to: worship, rituals, customs, and practices of US military personnel, international forces, and the indigenous population; as well as the impact of military operations on the religious and humanitarian dynamics in the operational area. (Approved for incorporation into JP 1-02.)

religious affairs. The combination of religious support and religious advisement. (JP 1-02. SOURCE: JP 1-05)

religious support. Chaplain-facilitated free exercise of religion through worship, religious and pastoral counseling services, ceremonial honors for the fallen, crisis intervention, and advice to the commander on ethical and moral issues, and morale as affected by religion. Also called **RS.** (Approved for incorporation into JP 1-02.)

religious support plan. None. (Approved for removal from JP 1-02.)

religious support team. A team, comprised of at least one chaplain and one enlisted support person, that works together in designing, implementing, and executing the command religious program. Also called **RST.** (Approved for incorporation into JP 1-02.)

Intentionally Blank

JOINT DOCTRINE PUBLICATIONS HIERARCHY

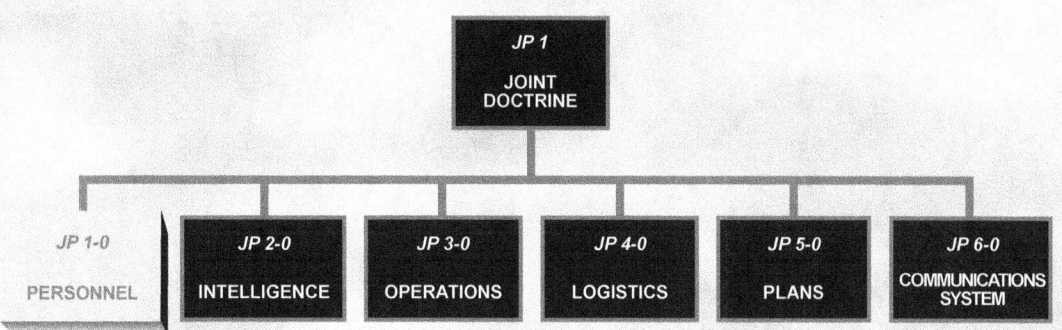

			JP 1 **JOINT** **DOCTRINE**		

JP 1-0 PERSONNEL	JP 2-0 INTELLIGENCE	JP 3-0 OPERATIONS	JP 4-0 LOGISTICS	JP 5-0 PLANS	JP 6-0 COMMUNICATIONS SYSTEM

All joint publications are organized into a comprehensive hierarchy as shown in the chart above. **Joint Publication (JP) 1-05** is in the **Personnel** series of joint doctrine publications. The diagram below illustrates an overview of the development process:

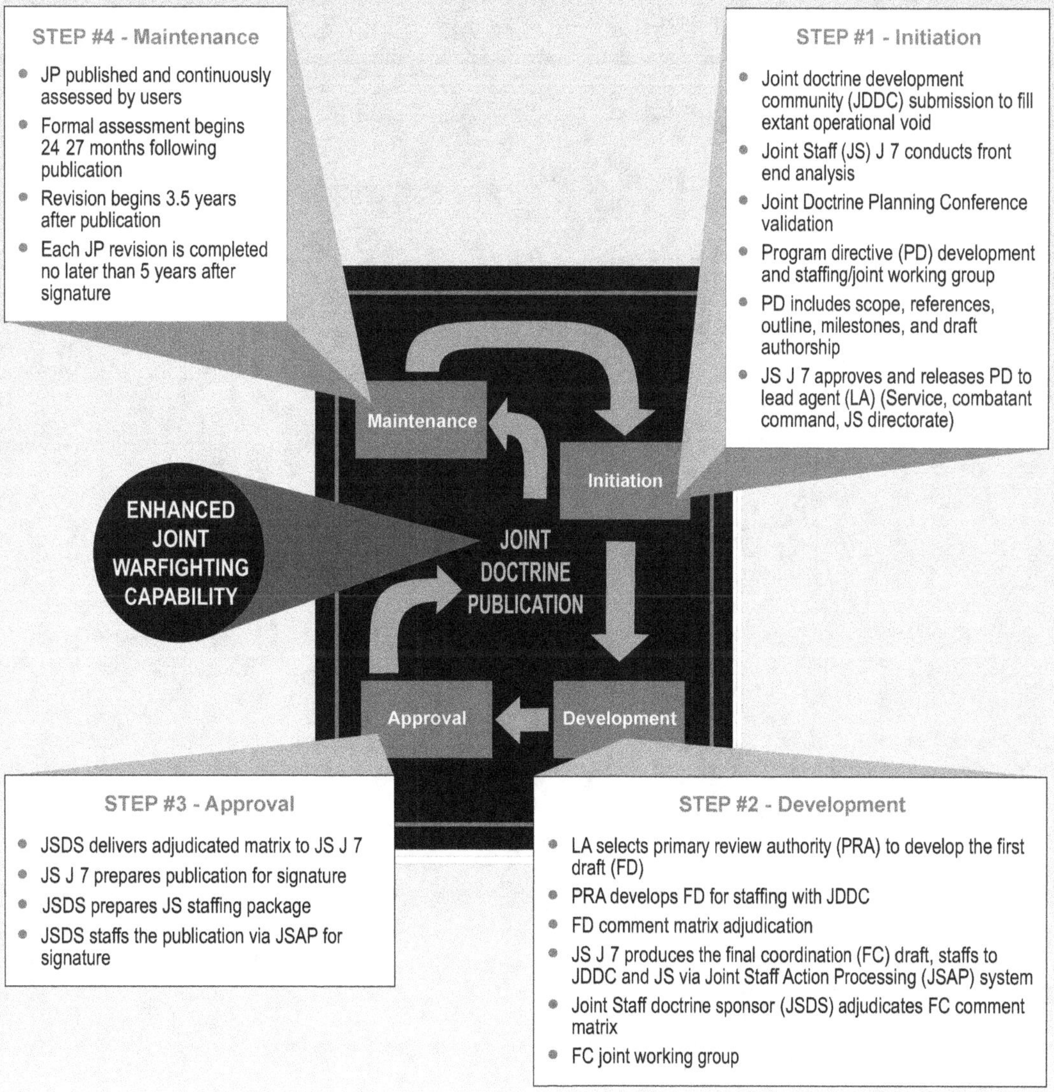

STEP #4 - Maintenance

- JP published and continuously assessed by users
- Formal assessment begins 24 27 months following publication
- Revision begins 3.5 years after publication
- Each JP revision is completed no later than 5 years after signature

STEP #1 - Initiation

- Joint doctrine development community (JDDC) submission to fill extant operational void
- Joint Staff (JS) J 7 conducts front end analysis
- Joint Doctrine Planning Conference validation
- Program directive (PD) development and staffing/joint working group
- PD includes scope, references, outline, milestones, and draft authorship
- JS J 7 approves and releases PD to lead agent (LA) (Service, combatant command, JS directorate)

ENHANCED JOINT WARFIGHTING CAPABILITY

Maintenance

Initiation

JOINT DOCTRINE PUBLICATION

Approval

Development

STEP #3 - Approval

- JSDS delivers adjudicated matrix to JS J 7
- JS J 7 prepares publication for signature
- JSDS prepares JS staffing package
- JSDS staffs the publication via JSAP for signature

STEP #2 - Development

- LA selects primary review authority (PRA) to develop the first draft (FD)
- PRA develops FD for staffing with JDDC
- FD comment matrix adjudication
- JS J 7 produces the final coordination (FC) draft, staffs to JDDC and JS via Joint Staff Action Processing (JSAP) system
- Joint Staff doctrine sponsor (JSDS) adjudicates FC comment matrix
- FC joint working group